D1744052

GCSE
English
Talking and
Listening

Evelyn Shaw

**Colourpoint
Educational**

6 5 4 3 2 1

© Evelyn Shaw
   2004

Designed by Colourpoint Books
Printed by The Universities Press (Belfast) Ltd

ISBN 1 904242 19 7

Colourpoint Books
Colourpoint House
Jubilee Business Park
21 Jubilee Road
Newtownards
County Down
Northern Ireland
BT23 4YH

Tel: 028 9182 0505
Fax: 028 9182 1900
E-mail: info@colourpoint.co.uk
Web-site: www.colourpoint.co.uk

Evelyn Shaw has been closely involved in preparing materials for teaching and assessing *Talking and Listening* for many years.

She is Principal Moderator with CCEA for GCSE English *Talking and Listening*.

In addition she has had a life long career in teaching and was Head of English in Regent House School, Newtownards. She has also lectured part time in Stranmillis University College.

Contents

Introduction

To most people it probably seems that *Talking and Listening* has been around forever – and in one respect this is true, for talking and listening are basic skills required for human communication. In an examination context, however, they are relative newcomers. In 1988, 'Oral English', as it was then called, became a compulsory part of GCSE English, long after reading and writing were accepted examination components.

One reason for the introduction of Oral English was pressure from the world of work. Employers wanted to be sure that the people they recruited with GCSE English qualifications would be as competent in speech as their exam results indicated they were in reading and writing. This requirement still exists and therefore *Talking and Listening* is now an integral part of English studies.

Currently, *Talking and Listening* coursework is worth 20% of the final GCSE mark. It is worth remembering that this is the same percentage weighting as is given to *Reading and Writing* written coursework. Consequently, in the short term, it is important that talking and listening skills are as well developed as possible to ensure a good GCSE grade. In the long term, being able to listen attentively and talk in an articulate and confident manner is a valuable asset in any sphere of employment or life.

This book is designed for students undertaking GCSE English. Many of the points made may seem rather obvious and the advice overly simple. Nevertheless, fifteen years of experience in moderating *Talking and Listening* would suggest that, while many pupils are well aware of the complexities of purposeful talking and listening, others still lack confidence and may appreciate help from any source.

Each section deals with one of the three forms of speech required for assessment – Individual extended contributions, Group interaction and Drama-focused activities.

Also provided are suggestions for practice to cover the range of competencies – explain, describe, narrate; explore, analyse, imagine; discuss, argue, persuade – in a variety of formal and informal situations.

I am indebted to my colleagues in teaching and on the CCEA *Talking and Listening* Moderation team for many of these suggestions which have been used in GCSE Moderation over the last years.

Where reference is made to specific texts, these have been selected from those most often featuring in GCSE English Literature courses and are given as suggestions only.

To all those who are in the middle of GCSE studies, the best advice still is to think before you speak and say what you have to say with grace and style. You do not want to be in that category derided by William Drummond in the 17th century:

> "But far more numerous was the herd of such,
> Who think too little, and who talk too much."

Individual Talk

A

"I did my work experience in a … em … like in an office. It was in … ahm … well it was connected with a big supermarket. The office had different parts … like some dealt with stock keeping and things like that. But I didn't work in that part. I was in the wages bit. The people I worked with were … em … like old fashioned. They didn't like me listening to my head set and stuff like that. Ahm … the work was OK … it wasn't hard or anything. But it put me right off working in an office. It was dead boring"

B

"My work experience was in an office connected with a large supermarket. The office had a number of sections; for example, one dealt with stock keeping, but I worked in the wages department. The other people in my section were rather old fashioned and did not approve of me listening to my head set. The work was not difficult but I found it rather boring and I have decided that I do not want a career in this kind of employment"

One of the extracts above was spoken, one was written.
Which is which?
What are the main differences?
Why do these differences exist?
What changes would you make to the spoken report? Why?

Have you ever heard yourself speaking on a tape recording? Have you ever seen yourself talking on video? It can be an embarrassing experience, but everybody can improve and, with practice, even the most stumbling speaker can have the confidence to speak with ease.

The type of talking we are going to discuss in this section is described in GCSE specifications as **Individual Extended Contribution**. We need to consider what this means.

Individual. This means that this should be a solo talk. There may be some questions or comments from your audience but the spotlight is really on you.

Some people enjoy being the centre of attention and have plenty of confidence so this kind of talk suits them perfectly. However, they have to be aware of their audience and be prepared to answer questions and challenges.

Other people hate being in the limelight and get very anxious if they have to talk in front of an audience. The secret to overcoming nerves is to be prepared. This section is to help everyone – both the assured and the worried – to make an interesting and effective speech.

Extended. This means that your talk should be of reasonable length. It should be more than a few comments and you should include depth of detail and develop your ideas, not just list them.

The prepared talk

This is the most obvious form of individual presentation and the one with which most of us are very familiar. In our daily lives we are surrounded by examples of public speakers making individual presentations – politicians, film stars, clergy, teachers, entertainers, heads of state.

Without realising it, you already know what you like and dislike about different speakers.

 Draw up a list of three speakers you like, and three you don't like.

Note what you like and dislike about their style of speaking.

This will help you when you are thinking about your own style of speaking and alert you to the mistakes which you will want to avoid.

"Why should I have to do this?"

Being able to stand up and talk in front of a small or larger group is a great asset in very many situations.

- You may plan to become a teacher or a salesperson or a cleric or a TV presenter or a politician.

- You may be in a job where you have to give a presentation on your project or a report to your bosses.

- You may have to go for an interview for a job.

- You may have to give a speech at a wedding or a talk to your sports club etc.

In many situations at work or in your leisure time, you could well be asked "to say a few words", so it is important to have the skills to do so with confidence and competence.

Stage 1: Preparation

Remember that writing a speech is *not* the same as writing an essay.

So when you are preparing your speech, you have to remember

Essay	Speech
An essay can be read and re-read.	A speech is heard only once.
An essay is written with no immediate audience in mind.	A speech has a very definite live audience in mind.

that it will be *heard* rather than *read* and that you have to make sure that it is interesting enough to keep your audience listening.

Here are four key points to remember when you are preparing the content of your speech.

1. Good organisation

(a) When you are preparing your speech, the first thing you need to do is gather together all the information you want to include and do any research you think is necessary.

For example, if you were asked to prepare a talk to promote a particular charity, eg NSPCC, you could collect leaflets, check their website, talk to someone involved with the charity etc.

(b) When you have collected all the information you need, then you need to decide what clear line of argument you want to present. For example, you might want to say that children at home need as much care as those in Third World countries. **Organise** all your information into the best possible sequence to present your argument.

Nothing annoys an audience more than a speech that seems to meander all over the place. It is so confused and difficult to follow that the listeners quickly lose interest.

2. An interesting opening

It is often said that the first thirty seconds of a speech are crucial. If the members of your audience are bored by your opening, it will be very difficult to win them back.

Rather than begin with a flat statement, such as "I am here today to talk to you about the NSPCC", you should try to think of a more interesting introduction.

For example:

(a) You could begin with a shocking or funny or interesting anecdote or story. For example, you could tell a story about the sufferings of a particular child.

(b) You could start with a personal comment. For example, talk about someone you know who has suffered abuse or explain why you have a personal interest in this charity.

(c) You could devise an unusual lead-in which would bring the audience to the topic from a surprising angle. For example, ask them to think about the amount of money they spent at the weekend. Perhaps get them to add it all up. Then tell them how much it would take to provide shelter for needy children, pointing out how a small sacrifice on their behalf could mean a great deal to these children.

3. Be rhetorical

In the Middle Ages the vast majority of people were unable to read. All the teaching, instruction and orders they received had to be given orally. So, if you were a person in authority and wanted to make sure that people would follow you into battle or learn new ways of managing your crops or follow your teaching in church, you had to be a persuasive speaker.

Consequently, if you were a boy of noble birth – in the male-dominated society of the time – who would grow up to be a leader, you would have learned rhetoric in school. The word 'rhetoric' comes from Greek and was defined as 'the study of the technique of using language effectively'.

Nowadays, of course, most people can read and write, but the techniques which these boys learned are still very helpful and are used widely. Here is a selection of some rhetorical devices which you could use in preparing a speech. It is not necessary to use all of them, but a sensible selection will give your speech a lot of impact.

(a) **Addressing your audience directly.** At the start and during your speech you should address your listeners:

"Fellow students …"

"Residents of Belfast …"

"Friends …"

"Ladies and Gentlemen …"

"Brothers and Sisters …"

or whatever is appropriate to your speech.

 Your aim is to make your audience feel involved and prepared to take a personal interest.

(b) Rhetorical questions. These are questions which don't expect a spoken answer or maybe have the answer built into them:

"Isn't it a shame that we can spend all that money on ourselves and think nothing of children dying in our towns?"

"What are you prepared to do help these children?"

"How much did you spend on junk food and drinks at the weekend?"

 Your aim is to provoke your listeners into thinking more carefully about your topic.

(c) Repetition. A key word or phrase can be repeated during your speech. Think of the impact Martin Luther King achieved by repeating "I have a dream today" in his great Civil Rights speech. You will find an extract from that speech later in this section as an illustration of dynamic public speaking.

 Your aim is to ensure that your listeners remember your key message and by remembering the repeated word or phrase or slogan, they will recall it.

(d) Alliteration. This means using the same letter at the beginning of words to emphasise your points. This can be in a phrase:

"Football is for the feeble"

"Soccer is for superheroes"

or it can be used to highlight key ideas during the course of your speech:

Misery; Money; Merriment

Carelessness; Caution; Cure

 Your aim is to help your listeners remember these important points and perhaps explain them to others.

(e) Imagery. Use metaphors and similes to make your speech more vivid and memorable.

"The mobile phone is the teenager's security blanket."

"Getting a new home was like a fairytale come true."

"If you buy your car from us, you will be driving a bargain."

 Your aim is to startle your listeners by the novelty of your imagery. It could be a lot more entertaining than those suggested here, and will make your listeners pay close attention to what you are saying.

(f) Emotive vocabulary. Use words which are designed to provoke an emotional response. This kind of language would seem over the top or over-emotional if you used it at length in an essay, but in a speech it can be used more freely and can sound very striking and persuasive. You might use words like: agony, misery, suffering, passion, freedom, triumph, ecstasy, glory etc.

 Your aim is to appeal to the emotions of your listeners and make them ready to agree with what you are suggesting.

(g) Bribes or threats. These, of course, should not be physical but clever verbal forms of persuasion.

"If you are prepared to back my proposal for a new shopping centre, I can promise you a whole world of exciting shops, along with great savings and 24 hour services."

"If you support this proposal for a shopping centre, you'd better be prepared for the hectic traffic, the litter and the non-stop noise pollution."

Your aim is to coax your listeners into accepting your point of view and to support your proposals.

(h) Variety in content and tone. This provides your audience with some light relief. A listener's attention span is very short, so it is important to include different ways of presenting your information and arguments. Some statistics can be included but do not over-do this as most audiences can only remember a few significant figures and will forget the others quickly.

You can break up the heavy information sections with some stories or personal anecdotes – the funnier the better – or you can illustrate some points with some moving, sad stories about your family or friends.

Geoffrey Chaucer wrote in the 1390s:
"For lewed peple loven tales olde;
Swiche thynges kan they wel reporte and holde"
which means:
"Ordinary people love old stories; things that they can easily retell to others and remember."

Modern audiences are just the same.

Your aim is to keep your audience listening by surprising them with unusual twists and turns in your talk.

4. A striking conclusion

You will need to build up to a high point at the end of your speech. We have already discussed the significance of the opening of your talk, but the conclusion is equally important. It is the last thing your listeners hear so it should be memorable. You should summarise your points at the end so they are in doubt about your message.

An old speechmaker's saying is:

"Tell them what you're going to say, tell them, and then tell them what you've told them."

You also need to prepare your audience, to alert them that you are coming to the end of your speech. Nothing is more embarrassing than the speaker who comes to the end of his speech and then stops. Nobody else realises that it is the end, so he is left standing in silence!

You can avoid this by guiding your audience in the final section of your speech by using phrases like:

"In conclusion, ladies and gentlemen ..."

"My final point to you today is ..."

"If you remember nothing else I have said today, please remember this ..."

"Above all else, remember this last message ..."

"Before I sit down, here's my final request".

Finally you should conclude your speech with an impressive phrase or words of encouragement or appeal.

Stage 2: Writing

You are now ready to write your speech. Here are two examples of master speechmakers at work. Read them and try to identify the various techniques they have used to appeal to their audiences.

The first is an extract from a famous speech made by the politician David Lloyd George in 1909. Quite simply he wanted the MPs to support his plan to introduce Old Age Pensions – but he had to persuade them.

> It is rather a shame for a rich country like ours – probably the richest country in the world, if not the richest the world has ever seen – that it should allow those who have toiled all their days to end in penury and possibly starvation. It is rather hard that an old workman should have to find his way to the gates of the tomb, bleeding and foot-sore, through the brambles and thorns of poverty. We will cut a new path through it, an easier one, a pleasanter one, through fields of waving corn. We are raising money to pay for the new road, aye, to widen it so that 200,000 paupers shall be able to join in the march. There are many in the country blessed by Providence with great wealth, and if there are amongst them men who grudge out of their riches a fair contribution towards the less fortunate of their fellow country men, they are shabby rich men.
>
> We propose to do more by means of the Budget. We are raising money to provide against the evils and the suffering that follow from unemployment. We are raising money for the purpose of assisting our great friendly societies to provide for the sick and the widows and orphans. We are providing money to enable us to develop the resources of our own land.
>
> I do not believe that any fair-minded man would challenge the justice and the fairness of the objects which we have in view in raising this money.

The second passage is from the speech made by Martin Luther King in 1963. He was speaking at a Civil Rights demonstration held in Washington to an audience of 250,000 people. His aim was to inspire his listeners, most of whom were black, and to make them believe that one day they would have equal civil rights with white people.

> I have a dream that my four little children will one day live in a nation where they are not judged by the colour of their skin but by the content of their character.

I have a dream today.

I have a dream that one day the state of Alabama, whose governor's lips are presently dripping with the words of interposition and nullification, will be transformed into a situation where little black boys and black girls will be able to join hands with little white boys and white girls and walk together as sisters and brothers.

I have a dream today.

I have a dream that one day every valley shall be exalted, every hill and mountain shall be made low, the rough places will be made plain, and the crooked places be made straight and the glory of the Lord shall be revealed and all flesh shall see it together.

This is our hope. This is the faith with which I return to the South. With this faith we will be able to hew out of the mountains of despair a stone of hope. With this faith we will be able to transform the jangling discords of our nation into a beautiful symphony of brotherhood. With this faith we will be able to work together, to pray together, to struggle together, to go to jail together, to stand up for freedom together knowing we will be free one day.

This will be the day when all of God's children will be able to sing with new meaning "My country 'tis of thee, sweet land of liberty, of thee I sing. Land where my father died, land of the pilgrim's pride, from every mountainside, let freedom ring."

And if America is to become a great nation this must become true. So let freedom ring from the prodigious hilltops of New Hampshire! Let freedom ring from the mighty mountains of New York! Let freedom ring from the heightening Alleghenies of Pennsylvania! Let freedom ring from the snow capped Rockies of Colorado! Let freedom ring from the curvaceous peaks of California! But not only that: let freedom ring from Stone Mountain of Georgia! Let freedom ring from every hill and molehill of Mississippi! From every mountainside, let freedom ring.

When we let freedom ring, when we let it ring from every village and every hamlet, from every state and every city, we will be able to speed up that day when all of God's children, black and white, Jews and Gentiles, Protestants and Catholics, will be able to join hands and sing in the words of the old Negro spiritual "Free at last! Free at last! Thank God almighty, we are free at last!"

Now, with your chosen topic in mind, follow through these steps so far, and write your speech.

Stage 3: Delivery

Cicero, the great Roman orator and writer, said there were five basic steps in speech making.

1. Decide exactly what to say.

2. Arrange the material in proper order with good judgement.

3. Clothe the speech in well chosen words and carefully phrased sentences.

4. Fix the speech in mind.

5. Deliver it with dignity and grace.

You have now taken steps 1 – 3, so you are ready to move on to 4 and 5.

Fix the speech in mind

Despite what Cicero said, it is not necessary to learn your speech off by heart. On the other hand, it is *not* acceptable to read your speech directly from the page.

Remember, you are being assessed for your talking and listening skills, not for reading.

You need to prepare your speech so that you are very familiar with it. To begin with, you will probably want to write it out in full. Then you need to transfer it into speaking notes.

Here are some questions often asked by students at this stage.

Q. Do I have to write out the whole speech?

A. No, but it will be very difficult to organise all your material in your head and think of how you will present it. Most people, even experienced politicians, need the discipline of writing out the speech to help them get control of what they want to say.

Q. Can I have my whole speech with me when I am talking?

*A. Yes. Some people like to have the whole speech with them because it makes them feel more confident and that is quite acceptable. **However,** they run the risk that they will lapse into simply reading the speech aloud.*

Q. What is wrong with just reading the speech?

A. The GCSE Criteria against which you are being assessed refers to candidates making: "attempts to engage the listeners' interest." (Grade E) and "sustaining the interest of the listeners through judgement in choice of style and delivery." (Grade C)

If you are keeping your eyes fixed on the page, you cannot be said to be engaging your listeners. You will simply be giving an exhibition of reading and that is not what is required here.

Q. If I write my whole speech out and take my eyes off it when I am talking, I'll not be able to find my place when I want to see what my next point is.

A. You should go through your speech and highlight or underline your main points, so you can spot them quickly when you glance down.

Q. If I don't want to have my whole speech with me, what is the alternative?

A. When you have gone through your speech and know it pretty well, write out a key sentence or bullet point for each paragraph or major stage. Have these key points with you and they should spark off your memory to recall the rest of your argument.

Q. Wouldn't I be better just to learn my speech off by heart?

A. This is not necessary. Apart from the fact that it will take a lot of your time, learning off by heart creates its own problems. For example, if you forget your words or forget the next point in your argument, you are stranded. You also run the risk of sounding too rehearsed.

Q. Should I have my speech or notes on A4 pages or what?

A. The best technique is to have your speech or notes on postcard-sized pieces of stiff paper or card. A4 pages are too large and can act as a barrier between you and your audience. In addition, when you are glancing down at your notes, it can be very difficult to find your place in a large page of writing.

A useful tactic is to put each major point on a separate card and have the cards in the right order so you simply have to glance at the next card to see where you are going.

Deliver it with dignity and grace

Now that you have prepared what you are going to say, you have to present your speech.

Some people find this a daunting prospect, but if you have prepared yourself carefully, you will be much more confident. Here are some issues to bear in mind.

1. Your eyes.

It is vital that you look at your listeners when you are talking to them, so you need to maintain **eye-contact**. Of course, you will want to glance at your cards, but you should do this as unobtrusively as possible. Hold your cards at a comfortable distance so that you can see them without bobbing your head up and down. For most people this will be about chest height.

Eye contact is essential for your audience to feel that you are communicating with them and that you are interested in their response. You should not just look at the walls or the ceiling or focus on one or two individuals. Try to look around at everyone so that each person feels you are talking to him or her.

2. Your voice.

Some people worry about their accent but this is not a problem and will not affect your assessment. Obviously, a student from Belfast will sound different from a student from Ballymena or Enniskillen or Newry, but local accents can be very appealing to an audience.

However, any unusual local colloquialisms should be avoided as they may not be understood.

Remember, however, that giving a talk would be classed as a formal task, so you will be expected to use correct grammar.

Grade D: candidates "are increasingly aware of the need of, and use of, standard English vocabulary and grammar".

Grade B: candidates "show effective use of standard English vocabulary and grammar in a range of situations".

You should make sure you understand fully how to use such commonly confused words such as:

did/done   saw/seen   went/gone

Your voice is your main tool for giving meaning and emphasis to your speech, so try to **vary your style** of speaking to avoid your voice becoming dull and uninteresting. In addition you should try to avoid any verbal mannerisms, such as repeated 'ahm.... em ....um', or repeating words like 'you know', 'like', 'sort of', 'stuff', 'I mean' etc.

The **volume** of your voice is important. It must be loud enough for everyone in the room to hear you, including the person in the back row. If you have a quiet voice, practise projecting it. At first, it may sound very loud in your ears, but remember you are talking to an audience, not a close friend. If you have a loud or high-pitched voice, you should be careful not to shout or sound screeching.

The **speed** of your delivery is also crucial. Nervousness often makes us talk rapidly and people in Northern Ireland have a natural tendency to talk very quickly, so it is very important that you make a definite effort to slow down. Your listeners hear your speech only once and if it is delivered at great speed, they will not be able to understand or remember it.

3. Your body language

It may not seem all that important to you, but **how you stand** and look at your audience can affect how they react to you. Think of the impressive and the not so impressive speakers you have watched!

If you prefer to stand still, then do so, but avoid standing so stiffly and rigidly that you look awkward and nervous.

If you prefer to move around a little, then do so, but don't be continually moving around or you will make your audience dizzy and distracted.

If you want to use hand gestures, then do so, but don't swing your arms around like a windmill or you will look ridiculous.

Nothing you do should take away from your speech, so avoid extremes. You should **try to relax** as much as possible, but don't become too casual or your audience may think that you do not respect them or that you are not taking the task seriously.

Physical mannerisms can also be very distracting. Habits like pushing your hair back repeatedly, swaying when you talk, rubbing your face etc, are very common. Check if you have any of these mannerisms and make a definite effort to avoid them when you are speaking. Any repeated random actions like these detract attention from your speech and your major points could be missed as your audience counts up the number of times you have pulled your ear!

It can be very helpful to rehearse your speech in front of a mirror or to have yourself recorded on video.

 *Q. "I am very nervous and couldn't face making a speech in front of all my class. Do I have do this?"*

A. Everyone doing GCSE English has to do at least one Individual Extended Contribution but it does not have to be this kind of formal speech. Others will be discussed later in this section. If you choose to do this kind of task, it is not essential that you deliver it in front of the whole class. On most occasions this is the type of arrangement which teachers use, but if you would find this impossible, then you can ask to have only a small audience of a few friends.

After the talk

After you have finished talking, it is a good idea to allow a little time for your audience to ask you a few questions or request more explanation. This allows you to show your knowledge and also fulfil the GCSE requirements.

Grade C: candidates "answer questions using relevant and effective detail".

Grade A: candidates "respond to questions in a way which is precisely matched to context".

Many people prefer this question and answer session as they can relax and talk more directly to their audience.

Other kinds of individual extended contribution

As well as the straightforward talk which has been discussed, you can fulfil the GCSE requirements in some other ways.

(a) After a group discussion, you can be nominated **to report back** to the class on your group's conclusions. Various forms of group discussion will be considered later, but as far as the individual talk is concerned, this report presenting the views of the group is an acceptable task.

(b) You can be a main **speaker in a debate**, presenting arguments for or against a topic.

(c) You can be a **member of a panel** presenting your particular viewpoint on a problem issue.

(d) You can **role play a character**, for example from a literature text, and present your opinions and ideas.

These are some suggestions. You can probably think of more. The important points to bear in mind are that you are talking on your own and at some length.

Suggestions for practice

Under the GCSE criteria there are three different groups of talk listed:

1   Explain, describe, narrate
2   Explore, analyse, imagine
3   Discuss, argue, persuade

The suggested tasks given here are designed to cover all these groups, but you are not required to cover them all in the Individual Extended Contribution.

Explain, describe, narrate

A talk on an area of interest. This could be on a hobby or sport, a part time job or work experience, a holiday destination etc.
Bear in mind that, if you are hoping to get a Grade B or above, you have to 'manage challenging subject matter effectively' so a talk on, for example, a personal hobby would not be considered 'challenging' enough. You will need to choose something more demanding.

For example:

- a presentation to prospective students explaining the benefits of a particular course;

- a talk on your local area, explaining its tourist potential;

- a talk to your class, explaining how you would stage a scene from a play you have studied.

Explanation of a specific process. This could be an explanation of, for example, how to train a children's football team or how you would teach someone to swim or how you would plan a trip to London etc.

 Remember that, if you are aiming for a high grade, you need to explain something more complicated.

For example:

- an explanation of how you would prepare a promotional video for your school or college;

- an explanation for young voters of the electoral system in Northern Ireland;

- an explanation of how you compose music.

A Review. This can be a description or review of a film, book, sporting event, musical event, TV programme, etc. The range of your vocabulary and depth of detail will largely determine your grade. You could do this as a straight talk to the class or as a mock TV programme presentation.

Promote a charity. You could choose a charity which interests you or with which you have had some experience: for example working in a charity shop. After you have done some research, you could explain the work of the charity and describe what it hopes to achieve.

As the GCSE specification requires you to 'interact in a formal situation', you will need to allow time for your audience to ask you questions on any of these topics. How you respond to these questions will affect your grading.

Explore, analyse, imagine

Reporting back. After you and your group have explored an issue, you could be nominated, or you could volunteer, to report the views of your group to the class. You will have to summarise the views of the group and defend their conclusions. To do this you will need to:

- make notes during the discussion;
- analyse the arguments;
- check that you are presenting their ideas accurately.

In the Group Discussion section of this book you will find suggestions for group discussions and you should practise being the reporter and answering queries from the other members of the class (ie interacting).

Role playing/Imagining. Either as a solo presentation or as a member of a panel, you can assume a role and explore and present that character's point of view. Here are some ideas.

- Imagine you are Lady Macbeth near the end of her life and you are giving her story of the events since her husband met the witches.
- Imagine you are Ralph from *Lord of the Flies*. Ten years after the events on the island, you are giving a talk on your experiences.
- Imagine you are a keen environmentalist making your statement as a panel member on a TV programme discussing a building or project which will affect your area. For example:

    lignite mining in Co Antrim;

    a new supermarket building on the outskirts of Belfast;

    a theme park building at the Giant's Causeway.

You could, of course, assume the role of another speaker with whom you would have more sympathy.

Be the teacher! For the class, explore and analyse a topic of your choice. Here are some ideas:

- Take a character from a book and analyse his or her personality and behaviour.
- Take an episode from a play or novel and explore its importance to the book as a whole.
- Take a topic from another subject in school and explore its importance and value for you.

    You could use visual aids or handouts as support material, if you wish. Again, how you interact with your audience in all of these tasks will be important.

Discuss, argue, persuade

Speaking in a debate. This is the most straightforward form of arguing and persuading. It is probably best for you to be one of the main speakers, but if you speak at length from the floor, responding and adding to the points made by others, this is also acceptable as an Individual Extended Contribution.

There are countless topics on which you can debate. Often the most successful are those linked to issues currently in the news.

Some perennial favourites are:

This House believes: a woman can never be too rich or too thin.
that fashion is for the feeble minded.
that charity begins at home.
that school uniform should be abolished.
that sport causes more trouble than it's worth.
that marriage is an out-dated institution.
there is no such thing as a just war.
that animals should never be used for experimentation.

Giving a talk on a controversial subject. This is similar in some ways to the debate speech, but without the debate formalities. You will be challenged here not by other speakers, but directly by members of the audience. You should present a strong point of view with the aim of persuading your audience to accept your arguments. The more controversial your subject, the better the reaction you will get.

You could propose a change to the existing law so that:
no-one under the age of 25 would be allowed to drive a car.
the death penalty would be re-introduced.
alcohol would be declared an illegal drug.
no immigrants would be allowed into Northern Ireland.
abortion would be banned.
smokers would not be allowed NHS treatment.

Be a politician. You could choose an existing political party or make up one of your own and give an election speech in which you discuss your policies and persuade your audience to vote for you. This can be very serious or, if you invent a comic party of your own, it can be very humorous.

Be an advertiser. You could invent a new product and give a speech promoting it. You will need to use very persuasive language and be as creative as possible.

Your product can have serious use:
    a new security device for old people.
    a speed restriction fitting for all cars.

Or it can be totally crazy:
    a net-seeking football.
    a miracle car which runs on water.
    edible cutlery for use on aircraft.
    a robot to carry schoolbags.

Your aim is to get your listeners to buy your product so you need to develop your concept fully and be prepared for all their questions.

In all of these tasks you will be demonstrating that you can "promote a point of view" (Grade C)

These are all suggestions which you can use in making your individual presentation. Many other ideas can grow from other work which your class has undertaken. The more often you take the opportunity to speak on your own, the more confident you become and the more organised and well-expressed your speeches become.

If you take time to prepare what you are going to say, you will surprise yourself with your performance, even if you are shy and feel nervous.

Group Discussion

Being able to contribute usefully in a group discussion is a very valuable skill. In many jobs, decisions are made through and after discussion; for example, whether:

> to release that CD
> or to accept a pay deal
> or to change the staff uniform etc.

In this section of Talking and Listening, the emphasis is not on solo performance but on your interaction in a group – on how you engage in discussion.

Talking in a group might seem such an obvious thing to do. Everybody talks on the buses, in the dining hall, in the corridors, on their phone.

There is a difference, however, between chatting and "concentrating in discussion and making useful contributions". (GCSE Grade E)

Swopping stories in a group is not the same as 'participating fully, sustaining listening and making significant contributions' (Grade C).

This kind of group interaction requires thoughtful discussion, careful listening and agreement on your way forward after sensible negotiation.

Possible problems

Without some thinking and planning in advance, group discussion can go terribly wrong. You must have seen, either in real life or on TV, discussions where one person dominates the talk and bullies everyone else into submission. This may be deliberate, to stop opposing arguments being made. Politicians are particularly keen on this tactic.

On the other hand, it might be that the person speaking feels passionately about his subject and gets carried away, forgetting that other people could have different points of view. Or again, this behaviour might be the result of a personality feature: the speaker is aggressive by nature and this carries through into his discussion.

However, it may be that nobody else is prepared to say anything, so this person does all the talking for them. Whether the fault lies with the individual or the group, this kind of conduct is not acceptable in GCSE discussion, or indeed in any civilised discussion.

Grade D General Criteria: 'candidates make a range of effective contributions, taking account of what others say'.

Grade B General Criteria: 'candidates should make an impact on discussion through sensitive listening'.

On the other hand, group discussion can get into difficulties if several – or all – of the members say little or nothing. They may listen quietly, nod in agreement and look interested, but they don't speak! It is vital to remember that Grade E requires candidates to 'make some contribution to discussion', so if you do not contribute, you cannot be graded.

Personalities differ and some people really enjoy the cut and thrust of discussion, while others find it rather intimidating. If you fall into the latter category, you should begin by making small contributions and build up your confidence with wider and longer comments as your GCSE course proceeds.

Organisation

Q. *What size does the group have to be?*

A. *There is nothing in the GCSE English Specification stipulating how many people constitute a 'group'. In most classes the usual number is six, but it is also possible to have paired discussion. However, it is important to realise that if you are aiming for a Grade C or above, you will need to show your ability to 'make probing contributions, structuring and organising points to achieve impact on the audience' (Grade B), so you will need a reasonably sized group in which to demonstrate your skills.*

Q. *Who should be in my group?*

A. *Most people find it easiest to talk with their friends and this is a good starting point. Once you have gained confidence, then it is best to discuss ideas with a wide range of people. By varying the membership of your group you will encounter different personalities and opinions which will add interest, and perhaps controversy, to your discussion.*

Q. *Do we have to have a chairperson, and, if so, what does he or she have to do?*

A. *The simple first answer is 'Yes'. A group which has no one in charge will lack direction and the discussion can become rambling and inconclusive. Before you start, you should decide who is to act as chairperson and then **accept that person's control**. During your GCSE course the role of chairperson should be rotated so that everyone has the opportunity to be in charge.*

The chairperson's job is to:

a) open the discussion by outlining the topic which the group is going to consider. If you are doing this in a formal situation, for example, a public meeting, then the chairperson should also welcome those present.

b) make sure the group remains focused on the given task. If anyone strays off the subject, the chairperson should diplomatically re-introduce the correct topic and move the discussion on with a new idea.

c) make sure the group completes all parts of the given task. In some situations a number of items may have to be decided. For example, you might be asked to draw up a series of programmes for a new radio station. In others, a single conclusion may have to be reached. For example, you have to decide whether or not an ex-prisoners' centre should be built in your village. Whatever the case, it is the chairperson's job to ensure that a decision is reached by the end of the discussion time. If the discussion appears to be getting stuck at any point and it seems that the group is in danger of not reaching a conclusion, then it is up to the chairperson to intervene and move the discussion on to the next point.

d) make sure everyone in the group participates satisfactorily. The chairperson should pay attention to all members of the group and if there is anyone who is not taking part, either because that person is shy or quietly spoken or because the discussion has been so hectic that he/she has not had a chance to speak, then the chairperson should make a point of inviting and encouraging that person to participate.

e) conclude the discussion. When all members have expressed their points of view and have reached a conclusion, the chairperson should summarise their arguments and announce their findings. If this has been a formal meeting, then it is usual for the chairperson to pronounce the meeting closed.

The discussion

Now that you have got your group organised, you can get the discussion going. You will be given a topic for discussion so you should look carefully at its exact requirements. Unlike the Individual Extended Contribution, this assignment should need very little advance preparation as the emphasis is on how you interact and react to other people's comments. In some situations – for example if you were asked to discuss which character in *Romeo and Juliet* most deserved your sympathy – you could do some background reading. On most occasions, however, you will be discussing and negotiating as you go, so you should be expecting your ideas to be changed.

 On no account should your group rehearse the discussion before your teacher assesses you. A series of mini-speeches is not a discussion and a rehearsed discussion always sounds stilted and lacks real, essential spontaneity.

In essence, the GCSE Criteria require you to show **two** main skills:

1. The ability to listen and engage with other group members.
2. The ability to engage with the purpose of the task.

1. The ability to listen and engage with other group members

Most of the major points to remember have been referred to already. To recap:

a) "the ability to listen" means exactly that! You may have strong views on a subject eg euthanasia, but you must listen carefully to what others are saying and give them space to speak. Listening implies more than simply not speaking. It means that you are paying attention to what is being said and this will be clear in how you respond. For example, you might say:

"I understand what you mean, Mary, about moral blackmail, but don't you think ..."

"Paul and Noel seem to think that old people are stupid but I don't agree because ..."

"That was a good point Lucy made about doctors' responsibilities ..."

b) "The ability to engage with other group members." If you have listened sensitively as discussed above, then you can take on board the viewpoints expressed by others and either develop them or challenge them.

Remember –

- You should try to 'engage' at different times with all of the group members and not just one or two. The discussion should not turn into a dialogue with the rest of the group acting as an audience.

- You should participate as often as possible in a helpful manner.

- If you notice any group member who is being side lined, you should support him/her. For example, you might say:

"Lee, you've been in a hospital on work experience. What would you think?

"What do you think, Jack? Would you be willing to switch off the machine?"

- No matter how heated the discussion becomes, you should not try to shout each other down. One person should speak at a time and not try to overpower the others. If people cut in and talk over each other, any sense of a meaningful discussion is lost.

During your GCSE course you should make a definite effort to develop your listening skills and improve your ways of participating in a group discussion. The more practice you have with a variety of people, the more comfortable you will become in group situations.

2. The ability to engage with the purpose of the task

A meaningful discussion will always have a purpose.

In the workplace it could be about how much overtime the staff members are willing to work

In the sports club it could be about how the membership rules should be changed.

Likewise your GCSE type discussion will have a purpose or topic and you will be expected to 'engage' with it. In practice, what does this mean?

- If it is possible and if it is necessary, you should think about the the topic and do some research. For example, you could find out about the legislation affecting young people in part-time jobs, or you could do some background reading on animal experimentation.

- During the discussion you must keep to the central issues. This sounds so obvious, but often people stray off the point and get caught up in all sorts of side issues. While discussing these may be very interesting, you will not be engaging with 'the purpose of the task'.

- Your discussion will require you to reach some conclusions, so be sure to make some decisions and follow through all the issues mentioned in the discussion topic.

The teacher assessing you will need to have this evidence of engagement when deciding on your grading. For example, a Grade B candidate would be expected to 'make probing contributions, structuring and organising points to achieve impact on the audience'.

Suggestions for practice

Just like the Individual Extended Contribution, there are three different groups of talk:

1   Explain, describe, narrate

2   Explore, analyse, imagine

3   Discuss, argue, persuade

Most discussion tasks will fall into categories 2 and 3. It is likely that they will go beyond straightforward explanation and description into analysis and discussion, so they will not fit into category 1. Your 'explain, describe, narrate' tasks will probably be either Individual Extended Contributions or Drama Focused Activities. (See page 48)

Explore, analyse, imagine

Discussion of a poem from your GCSE course. Your group should be given – or you can devise – a series of questions about your poems which you want answered.

Grade D requires you to 'show some understanding of unfamiliar ideas'

Grade C requires you to 'respond with understanding to ideas of varying complexity' – so reading and discussing a poem in a group will give you all the opportunity to grapple with new ideas.

Discussion of a scene from a play you have read. This would also be suitable. Your discussion could focus on how you would stage the scene, for example the Trial Scene from *The Merchant of Venice* or the Banquet Scene from *Macbeth*.

In the same way, you could discuss a selection of advertisements for similar products, for example food or make-up or cars. Decide on how they achieve their impact.

Exploration of an issue on which you all may have varying viewpoints. Here are some examples.

1. 'Children no longer have a childhood. Today's society makes them grow up too quickly'

   As a group, explore your views on this statement and decide whether or not you agree with it.

   You should consider:
   - young people's TV and magazines
   - the demands of parents
   - media role models
   - any other issues you think are relevant

2. Mobile phones – would you ban them or bless them?

3. 'Television can no longer be regarded as safe entertainment or a safe source of information for young people. Young people are exposed to material which is too adult for them and in many cases inappropriate.'

   As a group do you agree with this statement and what changes, if any, would you make to the present TV programmes?

4. A recent press report stated that students in UK schools are sitting more exams than their European counterparts. Do you think that pupils are being over-examined?

   In your group analyse this issue and consider the following:

   - external exams (eg Key stages, GCSE etc)
   - school exams
   - content of the school curriculum
   - your personal experience
   - your suggestions for the future

5. 'The clothes make the man'. How important is fashion to you?

   As a group, analyse the importance of fashion. In making your assessment, consider such issues as:

   - the cost to yourself and others of being fashionable
   - the pressure to wear only designer clothes
   - the value of uniform
   - the practice of judging people by the clothes they wear

Discuss, argue, persuade

It is in this category that the majority of your group discussions will most easily fit.

Remember that to achieve a high grade, you will have to choose a topic which will be challenging enough for you to be able to demonstrate higher grade skills.

For example, Grade B requires candidates to:

- manage collaborative tasks
- challenge and build on points made by others
- make probing contributions, structuring and organising points to achieve impact on audience

Consequently, a simple task like planning a Form Room for Year 12 pupils will not be demanding enough as it will not provide opportunities for probing contributions or challenging points.

Problem solving activities Here your group is given an issue which you have to consider and on which you have to reach a decision. Below are some examples.

1. As a group of students, you have been appointed to submit proposals for creating 'The Ideal 21st Century School/College.' Your proposals should include ideas on:
   - buildings and facilities
   - the curriculum – what should be taught
   - personnel (ie teaching and other staff)
   - extra-curricular activities.

2. Your group has won a prize to go on a round-the-world trip of your choice and you are now meeting to make your plans. You should decide on:

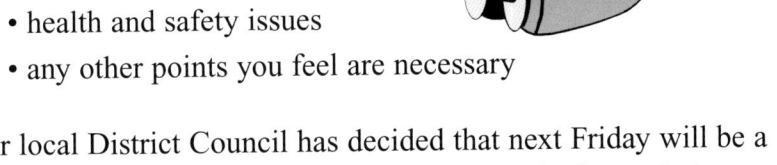

   - your destinations
   - your form of travel
   - clothing and equipment
   - health and safety issues
   - any other points you feel are necessary

3. Your local District Council has decided that next Friday will be a 'Green Day' when all motorised transport will be banned. As a group, do you agree with this plan and how will you cope?

   Discuss the impact of this on:

   - your family
   - your school/college
   - your neighbourhood.

Role Playing Often this type of discussion can best be done by role playing. This means that each person in the group assumes the role of an interested party and presents arguments from that person's point of view. Below are some examples.

1. In your neighbourhood, a grassy area has been zoned for development as a factory site. A public meeting has been called to discuss this matter and to decide whether or not to support the development.

   Present are:

   the builder/developer   a nearby houseowner
   an out-of-work teenager   a parent of small children
   a local shopkeeper   a teacher from the local school

2. The Government has decided to raise the driving age to 21. This is an attempt to reduce the number of accidents involving young people. Before the plan comes into effect there will be a public meeting of interested parties to discuss the matter.

Your group is made up of the following people:

a government spokesman (who is also the Chairperson)

a police Traffic Branch officer

a parent whose child was seriously injured by a teenage driver

a seventeen year old who is about to learn to drive

a car salesperson

a driving instructor

Explain your viewpoints and, as a group, decide on your conclusions regarding the new law.

3. The government has introduced a new law which states that all smokers and drug users will be denied free NHS medical treatment.

You are a panel of people brought together for a TV programme to discuss this issue. What are your conclusions?

On the panel are:

a parent of a drug addict who is now HIV+

a person who has been smoking since being in primary school

a representative of a cigarette manufacturing company

an ambulance driver

a doctor specialising in lung diseases

an elderly person who is waiting for a hip replacement operation

Discussions of controversial issues These discussions do not always require you to be in the role of another person. As a group, you can argue the plus and minus points of a whole range of issues and try to reach some consensus at the end.

This will give you the chance to 'engage with others' ideas, recognising assumptions and biases' (Grade C) and perhaps 'use language in a dynamic and influential way' (Grade A*)

Here are some suggested topics but the most effective discussions are often on up-to-date issues in the news.

- In China, no family is allowed to have more than one child. Have we ever the right to tell people to limit the size of their families?
- Has the Press become too powerful?
- Sport and politics should be kept strictly separate.
- Public money should not be spent on keeping museums and art galleries open.
- The only way to make vandals and hooligans behave is to use physical punishment.
- Vegetarianism is a lost cause.

Discussions leading to Reports This type of discussion has been mentioned in the Individual Talk section as the solo report at the end of the discussion would qualify as an Individual Extended Contribution. It is also valuable as a group interactive project. Your group will be given a task which will require a report or presentation to be made at the end.

Over the page are some examples.

1. Your group has been asked to organise an Anti-Bullying Week in your school or workplace.

   You should consider:

   • content: what will happen during the Anti-Bullying Week?

   • your target audience;

   • strategies for highlighting the issues;

   • evaluation: how will you decide whether or not the Anti-Bullying Week has been a success?

   At the end, summarise your conclusions for presentation to your Principal or Manager.

2. Vandalism in your area has led to the temporary closure of your local library. What steps would your group take to combat this vandalism? You should consider:

   • restricted hours of opening (ie open only during school hours);

   • employing security staff at the library, so using funds which could be spent on books;

   • only allowing people over 16 to enter the library;

   • any other ideas of your own.

   You should report your conclusions to the rest of the class.

3. Your group as a syndicate has just won £1.5 million in the National Lottery. How will you spend the money? You will need to decide:

   • how the money will be allocated. Will you keep it all together as 'group money' or will you share it out equally among group members?

   • as accurately as possible, how all the money will be used.

   Present your spending plan, and your reasons behind it, to your class.

4. Your group has been asked to draw up a programme of six lessons on Life Skills for your age group. You should consider:

- which topics must be included;

- which Departments in your school/college should be involved;

- which outside organisations should be involved;

- in what ways the lessons should be delivered.

Present your programme to the senior staff in your school or college.

Another crossover which will enable you to show either individual or group talking skills is the **Verbal Boxing Match**. In this format, you have two solo speakers – like two boxers – and each is backed up by a group of 'ringside' advisors. During the rounds (you can decide how long each should be) the individuals argue their points of view. During the breaks, (again the length can be decided) the group discusses the arguments so far and advises their 'boxer' on what could be said in the next round.

A well organised and thoughtful discussion of any kind can be extremely interesting and enjoyable. Skilled negotiators and effective managers have all developed their expertise in this kind of talking and listening so, as well as improving your GCSE grade, you will be enhancing your life skills by participating in group discussions.

Drama-focused Activities

Unlike the Individual Talk and the Group Discussion which were part of the Talking and Listening GCSE English syllabus from the start, Drama-focused Activities are relatively new. Consequently there may be some questions which still need answers.

Q *What exactly does 'Drama-focused Activities' mean?*

A *Put simply, this means that you, the individual candidate, have to assume a role other than yourself and you have to project and sustain that role or character.*

Q   *What is the value of this?*

A   *If you have read Harper Lee's* To Kill a Mockingbird, *you will remember what Atticus Finch told his daughter Scout – "If you learn a simple trick, Scout, you'll get along a lot better with all sorts of folks. You never really understand a person until you consider things from his point of view ... until you climb into his skin and walk around in it."
In a way, this is what you will be doing. By taking on the role of someone else, you will learn to appreciate the other person's point of view and to understand his or her behaviour. This is called empathising with someone.
In addition to developing empathy with other people, you will be extending your own powers of expression, both verbal and non-verbal. We will discuss this later.*

Q   *I'm no good at acting. Do I have to do this?*

A   *This is now part of the GCSE specifications, so all candidates have to be assessed in Drama-focused Activities. However, this does not mean that you have to act in a polished stage production in front of a large audience. There is a wide range of activities available to suit everyone from the very shy to the very confident and your audience can be quite small.*

Q   *Do I have to wear costume and make-up?*

A   *Again, your activity can be as formal or informal as you wish. If you want to be assessed in a full-blown stage performance, then you will be using costume and make-up. If your activity is impromptu and classroom based, then your requirements will be much simpler. You may not need any costume or make-up at all, but often the use of simple costume like a hat or scarf or glasses or coat, can help to make you feel more like your character.*

'Assuming a role' What does this mean?

In the Individual Extended Contribution and Group Interaction sections of your course, you may already have talked as someone else, for example as Malcolm being interviewed after the death of Macbeth, or in a role-playing discussion where you argued as a doctor opposed to abortion. However, in those situations you were being assessed on the skills described in Parts I and II:

Grade C: In Individual Extended Contributions, candidates adapt to different audiences, sustaining the interest of the listeners through judgement in choice of style and delivery.

In Group Interaction, they participate fully, sustaining their listening and making significant contributions.

In other words, the focus was on the content of your speech and how you presented it and on how you interacted with others in a group situation.

Here the focus is on how you present your character:

Grade C: In Drama-focused Activities, candidates develop and sustain a role effectively, holding the interest of the audience.

Of course, many of the tasks suggested for Individual Extended Contributions and Group Interaction can also be used for Drama-focused Activities such as the discussion on smokers and drug users. But the emphasis is now on how well you present your character – the doctor or the elderly person etc.

 Remember, the same task cannot be used for two assessments. You must opt for Individual Extended Contribution OR Group Interaction OR Drama-focused Activity.

'**Assuming a role**' means that, in addition to presenting your chosen character's point of view, you have to behave like that person. You will need to consider some techniques to convince your audience.

Language

What kind of vocabulary would this person use? Learned? Simple? Businesslike? Slang? Old-fashioned? Or what?

If you are role-playing a Shakespearean character, eg Shylock, you do not have to use Shakespearean language, but try to use the appropriate modern vocabulary.

Voice

Does your character have a distinctive accent?

At what volume will he/she speak? Loud, soft, moderate?

At what pace will he/she speak? Fast, slow, moderate?

What pitch of voice will he/she have? High, low, moderate?

What tone of voice will he/she use? Gentle, harsh, bossy, coaxing?

You do not have to be an impersonator, trying to replicate a voice exactly, but you should do your best to give something of the flavour of the character through the voice. To practise, you could record your voice trying out different modes of speech, or you could work with a partner, listening and advising each other on your quality of voice.

Facial expression

Try to visualise the face of your character and experiment with a mirror or a partner or a group to re-create facial expressions. You should concentrate on eyebrows, mouth and eyes and consider how they will change eg when under stress or when excited etc.

Gesture

Think of gestures which your character would use to express meaning or mood.

- the head – nodding, slumped, held high
- the hands – waving, twisting, clenched
- the fingers – pointing, tapping, fidgeting
- the shoulders – shrugging, drooping, held back
- the feet – shuffling, crossed neatly, held wide apart

Think of how your character would sit:

On the edge of the seat?

Very upright?

Sprawling?

Think of how your character would walk into a room:

Marching?

With short, timid steps?

Casually strolling?

Putting into practice

Take time to see how you can use all of these techniques to build up your assumed character. For practice, think of some of the figures from the books you have read and try to visualise and hear them. When you have done that, select some of their speeches and practise talking and moving like them.

For example, you could consider one of the following, or another character from one of your GCSE texts, in a crucial situation:

Bob Ewell	*To Kill a Mockingbird*
Simon	*Lord of the Flies*
Curley's wife	*Of Mice and Men*
Atahuallpa	*The Royal Hunt of the Sun*
Simon Stimson	*Our Town*
Shylock	*Merchant of Venice*
Tybalt	*Romeo and Juliet*
Lady Macbeth	*Macbeth*

If you are creating a character without any background information, then you will need to think carefully about him/her in advance.

For practice, select one of the following:

• an angry parent whose son has damaged the car
• a shopper accused of theft
• a cyclist knocked off his bike
• a traveller stranded at a railway station

How would each speak, walk, stand, look etc?

Miming is useful in helping you to explore a character and his or her reactions to a situation.

'Projecting and sustaining a role'. What does this mean?

Once you have assumed the role of your chosen character, the next stage is to present the character in some sort of situation where he or she can be fully appreciated – and assessed.

In this way your character is being projected or moved forward and developed. Your ability to sustain the role will be evident in the way you continue to think, speak, look and move in character.

The GCSE Criteria state:

Grade E   In drama -focused activities, candidates communicate with the audience by attempting to sustain a straightforward role through speech, movement and gesture.

Grade B   In drama- focused activities, they create a challenging role, shaping the audience's reactions through the use of different techniques etc.

Broadly speaking, there are two different kinds of drama-focused activity:

1. Improvisation ... which is unscripted

2. Acting ... which is pre-scripted

Improvisation

In the majority of classrooms, this is the kind of drama-focused activity most frequently used. Here students take on roles without any script and create their own characters. The characters are then involved in a variety of situations. The development of the storyline and the reactions of the characters are usually spontaneous but you can have some degree of preparation, if desired.

These improvisations can involve strategies such as hot-seating, thought-tracking, role-reversal or character transfer. Examples of these will be given in the 'Suggestions for Practice' section. In any of these situations, you will be interacting with your audience and other members of your group, so your listening skills will also be under scrutiny.

Acting

This involves using a text or scripted dialogue which you will have studied in some depth. This script can be a published one; for example, your Shakespeare play – or it can be one which you have written yourselves. You should be familiar with the action of the play and should discuss your part in advance with the other actors. In your performance, you should aim to present your character as convincingly as possible. Your listening skills will be evident in the way you understand and can communicate with your audience.

One of the criteria at Grade A and A* concerns 'the creation of a complex role'. How this can be achieved when Shakespeare, for example, has already created the role? If you bring your own interpretation of the role to your performance and it is evident that you are using originality and flair in your delivery, then the fact that the script was not written by you is not an issue.

Remember, however, that this cannot be just a reading exercise. You should either be performing without a script in your hand or with a script used only as a prompt.

Suggestions for practice

Again, the specific criteria in assessment are:

1. Explain, describe, narrate
2. Explore, analyse, imagine
3. Discuss, argue, persuade

The following suggestions could either be formal or informal tasks as your teacher decides on the complexity of the assignment.

Explain, describe, narrate

Hot-seating. In this type of assignment, a character is asked questions by other members of the class or group. In other words, they are put in the 'hot seat'. The replies must be made in role and, throughout the hot-seating, you must sustain that role.

Those asking the questions may or may not be in role, but you, in the hot-seat, must think and act as your assumed character and respond to the questions as your fictional persona would.

a) A character from a novel or play you have been reading is put in the hot-seat, for example Boo Radley, Juliet, Piggy.

b) You could be hot-seated as:

• a famous character from history.

• a modern celebrity.

• a character from a 'soap opera'.

• a person currently in the news etc.

c) A variation on this is to use a TV interview format with two people involved. The interviewer and the guest role-play their parts, with the guest being in the hot-seat.

Remember that at Grade C you should:

– use varied and appropriate vocabulary and expression

– answer questions using relevant and effective detail.

At Grade B you should:

– manage challenging subject matter effectively.

So be careful to select a character about whom you are well-informed and who has a fairly complex life and background.

Thought Tracking. This strategy allows you, in role, to say what you are thinking or feeling at a given moment in a play or dramatised version of a novel. For example, Lady Capulet could be asked to describe her feelings and thoughts when she finds Juliet dead, or similarly, George could be reflecting on his thoughts and feelings after he has killed Lennie.

This can be presented in the form of a monologue, followed by a question and answer session involving the audience.

Explore, analyse, imagine

Role Reversal. Here you should work with a partner who is also in role. At a given point in your play you should change roles with each other to explore the opposite viewpoint. For example, you could improvise a scene involving a Headteacher and a bullied child and half-way through you should reverse roles. Here are two more to try:

- a diner and a waiter when the wrong order has been served;

- a doorman and a teenager at a club with a strict dress code.

This exercise will allow you to 'respond with understanding to ideas of varying complexity' (Grade C)

Character transfer. The idea here is that a character is transferred to a situation other than the one being developed in the main improvisation or script. For example, he could be transferred to another time in his or her life. Keeping in role, you, as the character, have to improvise dialogue for the new situation.

For example, you could imagine and present:

- Lady Macbeth as a young girl when she has just met Macbeth for the first time;
- Shylock, one year after the famous trial;
- Christy Mahon living with his father before he attempts to kill him;
- Simon Stimson when he first came to Grover's Corners.

This could also be undertaken as a paired exercise with both people sustaining roles, eg:

- Ralph and Jack meet ten years later;
- Scout and Mayella Ewell meet when they are both grown up;
- George and Lennie as young boys;
- Jack and Simon at a choir rehearsal before they were evacuated.

This fulfils the GCSE criteria, 'candidates analyse and reflect effectively on real or imagined experience'.

Simulations of real life experiences. This activity is often used in many other subjects as well as English and is a helpful way to explore a difficult situation. In Drama-focused Activities, the emphasis is on creating and sustaining a role.

A range of issues can be explored from different points of view with each person in your group assuming the role of an interested party and presenting a piece of drama which explores and analyses causes, effects and solutions. Staying in role, you could also respond to questions from the audience.

- The Generation Gap. Improvise a scene where a group of young people meet an eccentric old man who tries to avoid them.
- Bullying. Improvise a scene where a very shy person is picked on at work by her boss.
- Modernisation. Improvise a scene where someone from abroad eg the United States, arrives in a remote village in Ireland and tries to change everything.
- Family conflict. Improvise a scene at breakfast time involving the family of a teenage girl who returned home very late the previous evening; or of the family of a teenage boy whose parents disapprove of his girlfriend.

TV-type Presentations. These can be loosely based on literature texts you have read or they can be wholly your own creation.

a) 'Jerry Springer' type show can be mounted with, for example,

- Macbeth and Lady Macbeth as the couple whose marriage is falling apart;
- Romeo and Juliet as the young couple whose parents won't allow them to meet.

b) An 'X-Files' type investigation into:

- the witchcraft stories surrounding the Macbeth royal family;
- the mysterious deaths of Romeo and Juliet.

c) 'This is Your Life' presentation for a major character
  • Atticus Finch
  • George Gibbs
  • Pizarro
  • Portia

To achieve a high grade, you will need to illustrate a good depth of understanding of the character you are playing and have the ability to convey that depth to your audience. As mentioned earlier, when presenting a Shakespearean character you are not expected to improvise in Shakespearean language, but you should find a suitable modern register of speech. For example, for the Duke in *The Merchant of Venice*, you would use calm, authoritative language.

Modern Re-writes. Instead of adopting roles from the plays and other texts, which you have read, you could adapt a situation from the text and explore how it would run if it were set in modern times.

  • After reading *Romeo and Juliet*, you could improvise or write your own script for a short play dealing with the issue of cross-cultural or cross-religious relationships.
  • After reading *The Merchant of Venice*, you could devise a play about a young man who is in dire need of money and has great difficulty in obtaining it.

In all of these strategies, the possibilities are enormous and with thought and imagination, you will be able to create many straightforward and more challenging roles to enable you to demonstrate your skills.

Discuss, argue, persuade

Many of the role-playing situations suggested in the Group Interaction section will be very suitable as Drama-focused Activities and will fulfill the Discuss, Argue, Persuade criteria. The emphasis, however, will be less on 'recognising others' opinions and responding appropriately' and much more on 'developing a credible role which engages the interest of the audience' (Grade D). In addition to these earlier suggestions, the following ideas could be developed:

a) A local heritage centre is in danger of being closed down. A group of interested people has been invited to appear on a local TV programme to discuss the future for the centre.

   Included are:

   TV Presenter

   Manager of the centre   Local MP

   School teacher   Building developer

b) There is a proposal to ban all private transport in your local town centre to encourage everyone to use public transport. A public meeting has been called to decide whether or not to proceed with this plan.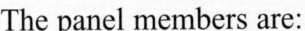

   The panel members are:

   a representative of the police

   a local shopkeeper

   a petrol station owner

   a public health official

   a local teenager

   the manager of the bus company

Remember in this task that the stress is on your presentation of a character, so you will need to construct a credible personality for your representative figure.

c) You could try out other formats such as a Late Night Talk Show with famous guests discussing topics of the day or a 'Parkinson' type interview with a controversial figure. You should aim to 'create a complex role', one who can also 'respond persuasively and engagingly'. (Grade A)

d) Court scenes work very well as Drama-Focused Activities and can grow out of other work, especially in literature.

- If you are studying a play, perhaps by Shakespeare, it can be very interesting to imagine what went on behind the action. What did Lady Macbeth's lady-in-waiting think about her mistress's marriage? What happened to the murderers? Then move from this stage to devise and present The Trial of Macbeth, (before he was beheaded), using the key figures in the witness box plus any background people you think are significant.

- You can adopt the same procedures to mount court scenes based on other texts. For example:
  - the trial of Jack after the boys return from the island
  - the trial of Count Dracula
  - the trial of George after the death of Lennie

• the trial of Pizarro when he returns to Spain

or indeed any other conflict situations.

An advantage of this kind of activity is that it can involve a great many people, including a Judge, Counsels for the Prosecution and the Defence, the Accused, a variety of Witnesses and other small parts such as Jurymen and Clerks (whose contribution would not really be sufficient for assessment). The main contributors should either base their presentations on the information contained in the text or create their characters eg as a Judge or Barrister, or a new witness, eg Piggy's aunt giving evidence about her nephew's state of health.

The important point is to 'create a challenging role … making probing contributions' (Grade B).

e) You could also choose to role-play an individual figure who is arguing the case on a variety of issues, both past and present. Having sought to persuade your audience, you should then invite them to question you, always sustaining your role.

For example, you could be:

- an Animal Rights campaigner arguing against the use of animals in all experimentation;

- a distressed parent arguing for heavy gaol sentences for all drunk drivers;

- an illegal immigrant trying to persuade the authorities to let him stay;

- a suffragette campaigning for women's rights;

- an anti-war campaigner in 1939;

- Sir Walter Raleigh trying to persuade men to go with him on his journey round the world.

Alternatively, you could choose to role-play a character from one of your texts who passionately believes in his or her cause. For example:

- Shylock arguing for Jewish rights;
- Atticus Finch arguing for equal rights for all citizens;
- Juliet arguing that love is more important than family obligations.

The overriding factors in all of these assignments are that you should 'develop and sustain a role effectively, holding the interest of the audience' and be able to 'promote a point of view' (Grade C).

Conclusion

For many people, this kind of Drama-Focused Activity could be more complicated than the more straightforward individual talk or group discussion.

If you are already studying Drama for GCSE or if you are involved with acting in the school, then you will encounter few difficulties.

If you do not have this extra experience, then you should aim to get as much practice as possible, but do not feel that an Oscar-like performance is required of you.

At the start, it is best to choose activities with which you feel comfortable and characters with whom you have some sympathy. As you gain experience, you can tackle more challenging situations and roles which are more complex and, perhaps, foreign to you.

Being able to assume a role can be very liberating as you are not talking and acting as yourself but as someone completely different. So you can be as outrageous or crazy as your role permits!